Using Emotional Intelligence To Lead

TERRI LOGAN, Ed.S.

Copyright © 2024 Terri Deann Logan

All rights reserved.

ISBN: **9798301898969**

DEDICATION

I dedicate this book to my mothers. Yes, mothers. I can almost say that the sum total of my life to date can be categorized as non-traditional.

To the mother who carried me, Carolyn Reed-Smith, Thank you. Thank you for showing me strength, for being my cheerleader, for being there for me and for my inherited fabulousness! I love you, mom....and I look just like her, ya'll. She is fierce, and I totally got it honest!! I will always remember your advice of always presenting myself well, because I never know what opportunity will present itself. Therefore, I choose and prefer to always be prepared! I appreciate you. Always.

To the mother who loved me like she carried me, Mary Nancy Logan, Thank you! Thank you for adopting me into your heart, thank you for showing me compassion and thank you for keeping me there, even after my father passed. I love you, mom. I can't say that many others would have continued to care the way that you do! A sign of true character, grace and integrity.
I appreciate you. Always.

CONTENTS

	Acknowledgments	i
1	Introduction	3
2	What is Emotional Intelligence?	4
3	Self-Awareness	8
4	Self-Regulation	10
5	Motivation	12
6	Empathy	14
7	Social Skill	16
8	Using Emotional Intelligence to Lead	18
9	Conclusion	28
10	References	29
11	About the Author	32

ACKNOWLEDGMENTS

I want to thank the educators at Georgia Southern University for pushing me to be a better writer. Math was always an area of strength for me. I assumed that my struggles with reading and writing were just my story. However, it was one professor who read one of my works and gave me an "F"! He gave me fortitude to step my game up! I am a bit of an overachiever, and I do not do "F's!" I appreciate the opportunity for the re-write and I thank you for the push.

I want to thank my big sister, Deirdra M. Reed, for being the springboard for my thoughts. I could always count on you to help me get through the writer's block, when I got stuck. I appreciate you. In those moments, I'm grateful for your capacity to hear what I wasn't saying and to help me articulate what I couldn't alone. Thank you!

INTRODUCTION

According to the Center for Creative Leadership (2024), leadership is defined as a social process that enables individuals to work together to achieve results that they could never achieve working alone. Merriam-Webster (2024) defines leadership in many ways, such as: the office or position of a leader, the capacity to lead or the act or an instance of leading. These definitions are wonderful and complement each other, but how does one take this information and apply that to the practice of working with people. Additionally, how does one become the type of leader that positively influences others and promotes organizational improvement? Knowing that leadership is a social process and relates to one's role is simply not enough information to act. Emotional Intelligence is the bridge between knowledge and application. Understanding the components of emotional intelligence and how they are applied, as you lead within an organization helps leaders improve their practice, relate to their employees and create a lasting impact.

WHAT IS EMOTIONAL INTELLIGENCE?

Leaders in decision-making roles are constantly faced with situations where the ability to recognize, understand and manage their emotions and empathize with others are necessary (Doe, Ndinguri, and Phipps, 2015). Though "intelligence" entails the capacity to comprehend information, "emotion" is a unified reaction to the environment (Ljungholm, 2014). Emotions play a central role in interpersonal relationships, due to their strong bearing on thoughts and behaviors (Dabke, 2016). In the early 1980's, Reuven Bar-On designed an instrument to examine the concept of emotional and social functioning. The emotional quotient inventory (EQi) was created to tell us more about emotionally and socially competent behavior and about the underlying construct of emotional and social intelligence (Bar-On and Parker, 2000). The term "emotional intelligence" was first coined by Salovey and Mayer in 1990 and later expanded and carried out to the world with Goleman's 1995 publication of *Emotional Intelligence*.

Maulding, Peters, Roberts, Leonard, & Sparkman (2012) found that individuals who demonstrated emotional intelligence and resilience, increased their leadership capacity; had a positive and profound impact on teacher efficacy and school culture; and ultimately created an environment which increased student achievement. Although this research relates to the instructional leader and the impact within a school organization, this information and the associated practices are equally applicable in any organizational setting. All leaders can gain insight in managing their human resources through this work. According to Brinia, Zimianiti & Panagiotopoulos (2014), an emotionally intelligent leader becomes a strong source of orientation and is the central point of reference for school life or within an organization. Doe, Ndinguri and Phipps (2015) found that emotional intelligence contributes to the success and failure of a leader.

The modern organization now holds a fundamental prerequisite of effective human resource development, which is best realized through effective educational or organizational leadership using emotional intelligence (Brinia, Zimianiti & Panagiotopoulos, 2014). But what is "emotional intelligence" and how is it successfully measured? Bar-On (2006) defined emotional-social intelligence as a cross-section of interrelated emotional and social competencies, skills and facilitators that determine how effectively we understand and express ourselves, understand and relate with others, and how we cope with daily demands.

Bar-On's model of emotional intelligence describes several competencies and their impact on intellectual behavior (Bar-On, 2006). Goleman (1995) detailed emotional intelligence as the ability to motivate one's self and persist in the face of frustrations. He explains that persons with emotional intelligence have the capacity to control impulse and delay gratification, as well as they are able to regulate their moods and keep distress from swamping the ability to think (Goleman, 1995). Finally, Goleman (1995) emphasizes the emotionally intelligent leader's ability to empathize and provide hope in others. In contrast to Bar-On's model, Goleman's model uses emotional intelligence to drive managerial performance (Bar-On, 2006). Salovey & Mayer (2004) offered a similar definition as the ability to monitor one's own and others' feelings and emotions, to discriminate among them and to use this information to guide one's thinking and actions. Salovey and Mayer's model provides an alternative view of emotional intelligence as a means to facilitate thinking (Bar-On, 2006).

Though the research of these leading authors, emotional intelligence can be argued to have four to five key elements (Bar-On, 2006; Goleman, 1995; Goleman, 2006; Salovey & Mayer, 2004). These elements play a key role in leadership style and development whether one chooses to acknowledge its relevance or not (Bar-On, 2006; Goleman, 1995;

Goleman, 2006; Salovey & Mayer, 2004). Despite the contrasting purposes from the perspective of leading researchers, emotional intelligence and its varied definitions reveal relevant and applicable processes mandatory to the work of effective educational and organizational leaders. So, let's discuss the attributes of emotional intelligence and those who possess them, a little more in detail.

SELF-AWARENESS

According to Goleman (1995), the first attribute of an emotionally intelligent leader is self-awareness. He discusses self-awareness as "the neutral mode that maintains self-reflectiveness even amidst turbulent emotions" (Goleman, 1995). Salovey & Mayer define self-awareness as "the ability to recognize a feeling as it happens." Bar-On (2006) discusses this component of emotional-social intelligence as the ability to recognize and understand one's emotions and feelings. Mayer states that self-awareness means being aware of both our feelings and our thoughts about those feelings (Goleman, 1995). The actions and behaviors of the leader are witnessed regularly throughout the daily operations of an organization, which supports the need for a leader to be self-aware. Emotionally intelligent individuals are more self-aware concerning their strengths and weakness, which allows for both the individual and the organization they serve to benefit from the bi-products of self-awareness: flexibility, swift reactions and innovation (change) (Ljungholm, 2014). This occurs because a leader who has emotional self-awareness is able to control their emotions; be assertive in their actions and rely on their own ideas with confidence. The final leadership behavior of self-awareness is that of self-fulfillment where the leader facilitates the achievement of personal goals.

"Intrapersonal skills" as defined by Brinia, Zimianiti & Panagiotopoulos (2014) relate to self-awareness as "the ability to understand deeper feelings, desires and ideas of one's self." The authors continuously state that the intrapersonal intelligence of school principals can be depicted in a grid of behaviors that includes self-esteem, emotional self-awareness, assertiveness, independence, and self-fulfillment (Brinia, Zimianiti & Panagiotopoulos, 2014). Stakeholders of an organization observe leaders in all of the above areas (Brinia, Zimianiti & Panagiotopoulos, 2014). According to Brinia, Zimianiti & Panagiotopoulos (2014), the leaders' ability to assert firm beliefs and a goal setting mindset can lead to the achievement of goals and overall acceptance by the staff. A leader who has self-esteem exhibits self-confidence, is positive and promotes a climate that employees like to work in.

SELF-REGULATION

The second attribute of emotional intelligence is self-regulation, which is defined as "the ability to handle feelings so they are appropriate" (Salovey & Mayer, 1990). Goleman (1995) states the goal of self-regulation is balance, not emotional suppression. He articulates how every feeling has its value and significance (Goleman, 1995). Bar-On (2006) discusses self-regulation as the ability to manage and control one's emotions, and adapt and solve problems of a personal nature. Another demonstration of self-regulation is the art of soothing ourselves which is a fundamental life skill (Goleman, 1995).

Managing one's emotions may help the leader to focus on problem-solving, empower the followers and create an atmosphere of enthusiasm and positive energy (Dabke, 2016). A sign of a leader's capacity for emotional self-regulation is the ability to recognize normal emotions of sadness, worry or anger and allow them to pass with time and patience (Goleman, 1995). The organizational leader who self-regulates shapes the culture in an indirect, intuitive and unconscious manner through modeling the appropriate way to manage one's emotions (Deal & Peterson, 1990). The principal is a teacher in the best sense of the word and supports teacher excellence through modeling appropriate behaviors (Deal & Peterson, 1990, Bolman & Deal, 2013). While this statement is specific to a school setting, the same holds true for any organization. The leaders of an organization are the models for the appropriate behavior expectations, in the organization. According to Brinia, Zimianiti & Panagiotopoulos (2014) the ability of the leader to deal with stress is central to emotional intelligence, as well as ensuring a stable and safe climate. Additionally, leaders can cultivate positive views of themselves and of others when they possess effective and strong intrapersonal qualities such as: exhibiting confidence in most situations encountered, adapting to the reality of the organization and being able to resolve problems by changing old habits in order to effectively follow developments and new conditions of the organization (Brinia, Zimianiti & Panagiotopoulos, 2014).

MOTIVATION

The third attribute of emotional intelligence is motivation. Salovey & Mayer (2004) define motivation or motivating oneself as the ability to marshal emotions, in the service of a goal. This ability is essential for paying attention, for self-motivation and mastery, and for creativity (Salovey & Mayer,2004). Bar-On (2006) discusses what could be best described as motivation as the ability to generate positive affect and be self-motivated. Goleman (1995) further discusses positive motivation as the marshaling of feelings like enthusiasm and confidence to enhance achievement. We are propelled to accomplishment due to the degree of which we are motivated by feelings of enthusiasm and pleasure in what we do or even by an optimal degree of anxiety (Goleman, 1995).

Motivation is not limited solely to the organizational leader, but it is an attribute that can be fostered, in others within the organization. Bolman & Deal (2013) articulate how the organizational leader can serve as a symbol or icon for others to admire or emulate. Dabke (2016) found that an emotionally intelligent leader needs to show affection, care for subordinates and show genuine commitment toward their growth as a way to foster motivation. Additionally, through support, to staff, students or employees, an emotionally intelligent leader earns respect, which in turn increases other's work ethic and commitment to the productivity of the organization (Dabke, 2016). A final best practice for increasing the motivation of others relies on the leader's willingness to provide help to and reinforcement for others, within the organization (Brinia, Zimianiti & Panagiotopoulos, 2014). By demonstrating a willingness to contribute time and guidance, a leader can increase the internal motivation of others. In doing so, the leader creates a culture of community and a climate of warmth which helps all stakeholders feel welcome and compelled to present their best self.

EMPATHY

The fourth attribute of emotional intelligence is empathy. Salovey & Mayer (2004) define empathy as the ability to comprehend another's feelings and to re-experience them oneself. As discussed by Bar-On (2006), empathy is the ability to understand how others feel and relate with them. Goleman (1995) expresses how the more aware or open one is to their own emotions, the more skilled one becomes in reading the feelings of others, or knowing how another feels. Goleman (1995) discusses the key to intuiting another's feelings as the ability to read non-verbal channels such as tone of voice, gesture, facial expressions. Goleman (1995) goes on to discuss the associated benefits of being a leader who expresses empathy as being better adjusted emotionally, more popular, more outgoing, and more sensitive. The benefits empower all leader to positively impact the relationships between themselves and the stakeholders of the organization.

Various daily interactions, within an organization, require empathy of and for all stakeholders. Assimilating emotion in thought, understanding subordinates with the help of emotions and judging or interpreting situations with the help of emotions are actions utilized by effective emotionally intelligent leaders (Hahn, Sabou, Toader & Radulescu, 2012). Being in tuned into theirs and others emotions better equips leaders to intervene in emotionally challenging situations through the use of individualized support, empathy and role modeling (Mathew & Gupta, 2015; Dabke, 2016). Brinia, Zimianiti & Panagiotopoulos (2014) articulate a key action of emotionally intelligent leaders as the ability to attentively listen to the ideas of subordinates, even when the leader disagrees. By utilizing empathy, leaders are more apt to understand their stakeholder's emotions and to effectively manage relationships within the organization (Doe, Ndinguri & Phipps, 2015).

SOCIAL SKILL

Social skill represents the fifth attribute of emotional intelligence. Salovey & Mayer (2004) define handling emotions or social skill as the skill in managing emotions of others. Bar-On (2006) discusses social skill as the ability to manage, change, adapt and solve problems of an interpersonal nature. Goleman (1995) discussed the importance of managing emotions in someone else when handling relationships. He defined social skill as the coordination of moods is the essence of rapport, and rapport as an emotional skill essential for the preservation of close relationships, whether in marriage, a friendship, or a business partnership (Goleman, 1995). In contrast, Bar-On and Parker (2000) discuss social intelligence as a set of purposive and strategic behaviors which are oriented toward the achievement of some purpose or goal. They articulate that these behaviors are inherently social and contextualized, in that all actions take place within a given cultural context in which actions take on socially defined meanings (Bar-on & Parker, 2000). Social intelligence, then, could be an alternate means to describe the social interactions necessary to effectively manage human resources.

While discussing organizational behavior, Ljungholm (2014)

states how the leader interacts emotionally with stakeholders is of fundamental importance. Additionally Dabke (2016), found that subordinates associate emotional intelligence with effectiveness and appreciate leaders who exhibit emotional intelligence. The effective emotionally intelligent leader connects smoothly with people and can adequately express their own feelings (Goleman, 1995; Kacmar, Andrews, Harris & Tepper, 2013). These leadership behaviors creates the capacity for a leader to shape an encounter through the astute reading of others' reactions and feelings, to lead, mobilize and inspire others, to thrive in intimate relationships, to persuade and influence, and to put others at ease when handling the disputes that are bound to flare up in any human activity (Goleman, 1995; Kacmar, Andrews, Harris & Tepper, 2013).

USING EMOTIONAL INTELLIGENCE TO LEAD

My journey in to leadership was non-traditional. In high school, I wanted to perform. I attended Spelman College as Women In Science and Engineering Scholar and learned that although I was the product of my father, who was an engineer, and my mother, who was an educator, I did not know where I truly fit. After spending some time waiting tables, I took a non-traditional route to become an educator. I taught math for several years, but one day realized that I needed more. Upon the encouragement of a new leader, I began to apply for assistant principal positions. I had taken and passed the necessary assessment and was qualified, but did not have the title to support that credential. Then one day it happened, and I got the call to interview for a coordinator position. So, once again through a very non-traditional process, I became the Coordinator of an alternative education program. I didn't have the training, I had not earned the degree, and the only experience that I had obtained was that of one year as a mathematics instructional coach. In that role, I supported the leadership team, but did not truly possess the duties and responsibilities of a leader.

I attribute much of my success to relying on emotional

intelligence, although at the time, I did not realize that was the coined term for how I engaged with others. Unlike the stoic examples in many text books, students, faculty and staff are not one dimensional letters on a page. They are "people with emotions" before they take on any other title and their lived experiences and their subsequent emotions have the ability to shape (and potentially derail) an instructional day. The emotionally intelligent leader embraces emotional intelligence as a framework for creating the positive learning environment and warm climate necessary to increase achievement.

As an organizational leader of a school, I have learned to practice self-awareness. Over the years, I have observed that I have the ability to "center" myself and prepare for the day ahead. This ritual consists of going to bed at a specific time; listening to music on my drive to work and keeping healthy snacks at school to nosh on throughout the day. These practices keep me balanced and able to address challenges within the building from a more neutral, less reactive place. I often walk the building throughout the day. My walks served many purposes. Sometimes, I used the time as a time to process the interactions that I have had with students, faculty and staff throughout the day. Whereas, other times I walk to handle the business of organizational management or to investigate a matter as it pertained to the discipline process. During some of my walks, I am able to detach from specific incidents and take time to judge the situation and make sure that the appropriate measures were taken to resolve the issue. If on my walk, I "unearth" that I may have mishandled a situation because for some reason I wasn't neutral. In those situations, I then go back and correct my actions. This was not always an easy practice, nor was it one that was modeled for me, but it proved to be extremely effective. Some view apologizing as weakness, but this is not my view. I am human, and I make mistakes. It took strength to admit my wrong and then take the necessary steps to rectify that behavior. I did so, regardless of whether it meant relating to a student, staff member, or any other relevant stakeholder. We all deserve respect. Therefore, as one who considers herself to be emotionally intelligent, I would go above and beyond to ensure that I was the model of respect, in our building.

Working in an urban district, I have seen and heard many unimaginable scenarios. I have come to believe that the art of self-regulation is an essential skill that must be mastered in order to be an effective leader. In my role as Coordinator, I was often called on to intervene in situations where a young person may have been disruptive to the learning environment. My title alone did not always ensure that the student would deescalate, upon my arrival. This could and would lead to me being disrespected, in some way. In one instance during the discipline process, a student called me an inappropriate name. I was livid, but did not respond in an unprofessional manner. Without a clear sense of self and the ability to self-regulate, the incident could have potentially spiraled out of control. But instead, I used the incident not only to practice self-regulation, but to model to the student that practicing self-regulation could have helped her avoid the incident, in the first place. I discussed with the young lady how she had allowed her anger to influence a negative behavior or outburst (Ljungholm, 2014). I continued by articulating some questions, to the student, that could have been a part of her "self-talk": For example, "Will fighting this person get you closer to your educational goals?", or "Do I want to get in trouble for someone that I don't even like?" After the conclusion of our conversation, the student was able to talk out her emotions and come to the realization that her actions, in anger, could have potentially derailed her education plan. We ended the conversation with her articulating to me what she could do, in the future, to make a different choice.

Effective leaders should consider the consequences of their decisions, especially the emotional impact that these decisions will have on the involved students, staff or employees (Doe, Ndinguri & Phipps, 2015). Though I try to practice self-regulation, I can recall an incident where I did not use self-regulation well. I encountered a classroom that was so loud that I could hear them down the hallway. When I approached the classroom door, I encountered a frazzled teacher who could barely be heard over the small sets of students conversing; the games being played and shared on cell phones and the students generally off task. Although, there were students who were trying to listen to the lesson, they were not the majority. Without asking permission from the teacher, I walked in, began to lecture the whole class on the importance of education and how their behavior was inappropriate. This rant went on for several minutes, and was a prime example of my not exercising self-regulation. Later, I was confronted by both the teacher and some of the students, about my behavior. The teacher felt my intervention was an over-step and might even be considered as micro-management. My behavior sent a poor signal to the students about her ability to control her classroom. The students who were on task felt like they were unfairly reprimanded, for behavior that they were not participating in. In hindsight, I realized that my actions were out of my own sense of frustration. I had not fully considered addressing the situation without taking over, in a way that would have dealt with the individuals misbehaving, while assisting the teacher. I further realized that a more appropriate way to handle the situation and a best practice that honored emotional intelligence, would have been to address the misbehaving students, in private setting, in an effort to be thoughtful of their emotions prior to correcting their behavior, while simultaneously leaving the teacher's classroom intact for instruction (Ljungholm, 2014). In this particular situation, I apologized to both the teacher and the students who felt wrongly reprimanded. I did so in front of the whole class, as that was the way that I had conducted the inappropriate behavior. Self-regulation takes practice to master. In this situation, I learned from my mistakes and improved my self-regulation efforts so that I would not repeat an incident of this nature.

In organizational leadership, motivation is essential. As an educational leader of an alternative school, motivation was paramount. Teenagers are my favorite group of students to work with. However, they don't always express appreciation for the work that must be done to create a positive learning environment. Therefore, having practices that motived myself was a part of what I did regularly. Also, they were often my motivation. They didn't always recognize when they had grown, or when they had mastered a new skill or gone to another level towards their ultimate goal, but as the person who was always watching, I did. This gave me motivation. My goal is help the people that I encounter be their best selves and reach their goals through positive workplace interactions. I model enthusiasm for our students and celebrate the successes that they have, as a testament to the hard work that teachers and staff do on a daily basis.

Having spent many hours in the classroom setting, I have been known as a person who will roll up my sleeves and pick up a piece of chalk, use an overhead projector…or a dry erase marker! During one observation, I noticed that the teacher had some instructional deficits and was struggling to articulate the concept to the class. After the observation, I scheduled a 1:1 conversation with the teacher; we talked about the trouble she was experiencing and tools she may be able to incorporate. We also made time for me to both model for her during her instructional time as well as address in a separate professional training with others as a "teachable moment". After the training, many teachers came and thanked me for the time that I spent helping address their frustration. They also discussed how knowing that they were in a "judgment free zone" helped foster their growth and inspired them to do more! Although not my duty or responsibility to perform in this manner, motivating myself to lend a hand to aid in the betterment of another is emotional intelligence in action.

In the workplace, empathy can sometimes be thrown by the way side in pursuit of "time on task". Ljungholm (2014) noted regulation and indication of emotions as a type of intelligence that has practical advantages, for the person in processes of social interplay. Leaders who demonstrate empathy in their organizational management have an impact that is far greater than they can imagine. This year, a student who had been at the school for more than two years came into the building visibly upset. Knowing this student, I asked if there was anything wrong. The student replied "no", but his body language said something differently. "You are not ready to learn." I told him and escorted him to the counselor's office. After speaking with the counselor, the student had had major issues at home and actually was in need of psychological care. The ability to empathize with the student coming into the building in tears and to comprehend their feelings and demonstrate empathy for those feelings (Salovey & Mayer, 2004) gave me the ability to step outside of the role of "administrator" and connect with the emotional well-being of the student, which could possibly be a turning point in their ultimate educational success. Showing empathy that day was freely given, and not easily forgotten.

Social skills are the final attribute of emotional intelligence and are the culmination of successfully managing all the other components. For an organizational leader, it is creating the environment that supports self-awareness, self-regulation, motivation and empathy as a "way of being". I work diligently to demonstrate all of the attributes of emotional intelligence, in all of my interactions. Creating a positive climate and culture, within your organization, can take time and it will definitely take work. To that end, the "judgment free zone" is for anyone who engages with the organization. My leadership role, at the time, was in a school; therefore, my audience was teachers, students, parents, staff, other district employees and community members. Everyone should feel welcome when they walk the halls of whatever organization for which I lead.

My personal style is to arm myself with stories from my life that serve as "parables" and ways to engage in a dialogue without anyone feeling like I am being condescending. Another strategy I utilize when working my social skills is to learn something about the person that I am engaging with through active listening, therefore, they feel connected to and with even if I do not have a lived experience comparable to theirs. I see the "whole person" and the "whole scenario" rather than a set of factors, in an incident. As it pertained to the faculty and staff, I made effort to pay real attention to them as an important and invaluable part of our organization. The idea that students may come to school from an environment that colors the way they enter the building has been a longstanding concern, but the way in which adults enter the building has been less acknowledged. I am a leader committed to creating an environment of success for all and have chosen to seek out ways to acknowledge the humanity of the individuals that I interact with each day. From "Good Morning", "how are you today" to appreciation days and co-teaching, I do the work to support those in my building. This work is not always completed by me alone, as I have teams of individuals who support me. You will too. I am a firm believer that teamwork makes the dream work. However, as the leader, we are the catalyst and the beginning of that team.

CONCLUSION

Emotional intelligence is a master aptitude, a capacity that profoundly affects all other abilities, either facilitating or interfering with them (Goleman, 1995). The emotionally intelligent leader who demonstrates the ability to be thoughtful, creative, flexible, appreciative, respectful and willing to learn from the diverse viewpoints of all stakeholders becomes a role model and builds the trust necessary to strengthen collaborative efforts (Maulding, Peters, Roberts, Leonard, & Sparkman, 2012; Brinia, Zimianiti & Panagiotopoulos, 2014). Emotions make us human and the education concerning the attributes of an emotional intelligent leader represents a worthwhile endeavor for all organizational leaders. Emotional intelligence is a necessary leadership component for good organizational human management and development. In fact, I believe that it is a mandatory component of good human practice. I truly believe that through a more intentional and widespread application of emotional intelligence the world would be a better place.

REFERENCES

Bar-On, R. (2006). The Bar-On model of emotional-social intelligence (ESI). *Psicothema, 18,* 13-25.

Bar-On, R. & Parker, J. (2000). *The handbook of emotional intelligence: Theory, development, assessment and application at home, school, and in the workplace.* San Francisco, GA: Jossey-Bass.

Bolman, L. G. & Deal, T. E. (2013). *Reframing organizations: Artistry, choice, and leadership.* San Francisco, CA: Jossey-Bass.

Brinia, V., Zimianiti, L. & Panagiotopoulos, K. (2014). The role of the principal's emotional intelligence in primary education leadership. *Educational Management Administration & Leadership, 42*(4), 28-44.

Center for Creative Leadership (2024) What is Leadership? https://www.ccl.org/articles/leading-effectively-articles/what-is-leadership-a-definition/ Retrieved on December 11, 2024.

Dabke, D. (2016). Impact of leader's emotional intelligence and transformational behavior on perceived leadership effectiveness: A multiple source view. *Business Perspectives & Research, 4*(1), 27-40. doi: 10.1177/2278533715606433

Deal, T. & Peterson, K. (1990). *The principal's role in shaping school culture.* Office of Educational Research and Improvement. U. S. Department of Education.

Doe, R., Ndinguri, E. & Phipps, S. A. (2015) Emotional intelligence: The link to success and failure of leadership. *Academy of Educational Leadership Journal, 19*(3), 105-114.

Goleman, D. (1995). *Emotional Intelligence.* New York, NY: Bantem Books.

Goleman, D. (2006). *Social Intelligence: The New Science of Human Relationships.* New York, NY: Bantem Books.

Hahn, R., Sabou, S., Toader, R. & Radulescu, C. M. (2012). About emotional intelligence and leadership. *Annals of the University of*

Oradea, Economic Science Series, 21(2), 744-749.

Kacmar, K., Andrews, M., Harris, K. & Tepper, B. (2013). Ethical leadership and subordinate outcomes: The mediating role of organizational politics and the moderating role of political skill. *Journal of Business Ethics, 115* (1), 33-44. Doi:10.1007/s10551-012-1373-8.

Ljungholm, D. P. (2014). Emotional intelligence in organizational behavior. *Economics, Management & Financial Markets, 9*(3), 128-133.

Maulding, W. S., Peters, G. B., Roberts, J., Leonard, E. & Sparkman, L. (2012). Emotional intelligence and resilience as predictors of leadership in school administrators. *Journal of Leadership Studies, 5*(4), 20-29. Doi: 10.1002/jls.20240

Merriam-Webster. www.merriam-webster.com retrieved on December 11, 2024.

Salovey, P., Brackett, M. & Mayer, J. (2004). *Emotional intelligence: Key readings on the Mayer and Salovey model.* Port Chester, New York: Dude Publishing.

ABOUT THE AUTHOR

Hello, I'm Terri. When I was young, I wanted to be an entertainer. I love performing on a stage, singing and dancing. I never thought that leadership would be a major part of my life. I had held small leadership roles such as co-captain of my dance team and parliamentarian of the SGA, but it was the role of Coordinator that made the difference. I discovered my purpose and my love for the process of leading people and improving organizations. There is no better feeling than working with people and watching your influence improve the organization and the lives of the people associated. I hope that my work helps you, as you help to improve our world. Thank you for your service and for your leadership.

I truly appreciate you taking your time to read my book.

Terri Deann Logan, Ed.S.
Leader, Author, Educator, and Content Creator
JustTerri180 on YouTube/TikTok
IG @terridlogan33

www.ingramcontent.com/pod-product-compliance
Lightning Source LLC
Chambersburg PA
CBHW070943220526
45469CB00007B/2500